Birds
Of Machu Picchu

8 6   m o s t   c o m m o n   s p e c i e s

written by
Gino Cassinelli Del Sante

illustrations by
Daniel Huaman Chang

revised by
Alfredo J. Begazo Dongo
Thomas Valqui Haase

Text and concept/Gino Cassinelli Del Sante

Production manager/Flavio Casalino

English version/Germán Gonzáles

Design/Gabriel Herrera

Photographs/Alejandro Balaguer

Map illustration/GGG

Pre-press/Litho Láser

Printing and binding/Metrocolor

Published by: Gino Cassinelli Del Sante

oreste@terra.com.pe

http://barrioperu.terra.com.pe/oreste

Copyright by: Gino Cassinelli Del Sante

Hecho el deposito legal: 1501082003-2248

ISBN 9972-9172-1-5

Registro de Derecho de autor (Indecopi)

N. de Partida registral 00421-2003

Se terminó de imprimir en el mes de julio de 2003
en los talleres gráficos de Metrocolor
Lima-Peru

Index

Introduction

THIS BOOK IS A FIELD GUIDE for the identification of the most commonly seen birds at the Machu Picchu Historical Sanctuary (MPHS). Rather than a scientific tratement of the bird-life in the sanctuary, it aims to provide accessible information to the laymen who are interested, in their own way and pace, about wildlife and nature.

Here, the reader will find 86 species chosen among the most colorful and the most common in the MPHS. Each one has a description of its main features, habits, behavior and other interesting facts.

To make identification easier, the 86 species have been classified in nine groups, according to their habitats or behavior.

To get an idea of the bird`s size, a scale silhouette shows each bird next to scale drawing of this book, which is 20.5 cm or 8 inch high. When dealing with species whose male and female individuals have different shapes or looks, the illustrations show the male, usually the most colorful and eye-catching one of the pair.

For those cases in which taxonomic classification is still being debated by ornithologists, it has been applied the one used by Ridgely and Tudor (2001) in "The Birds of South America".

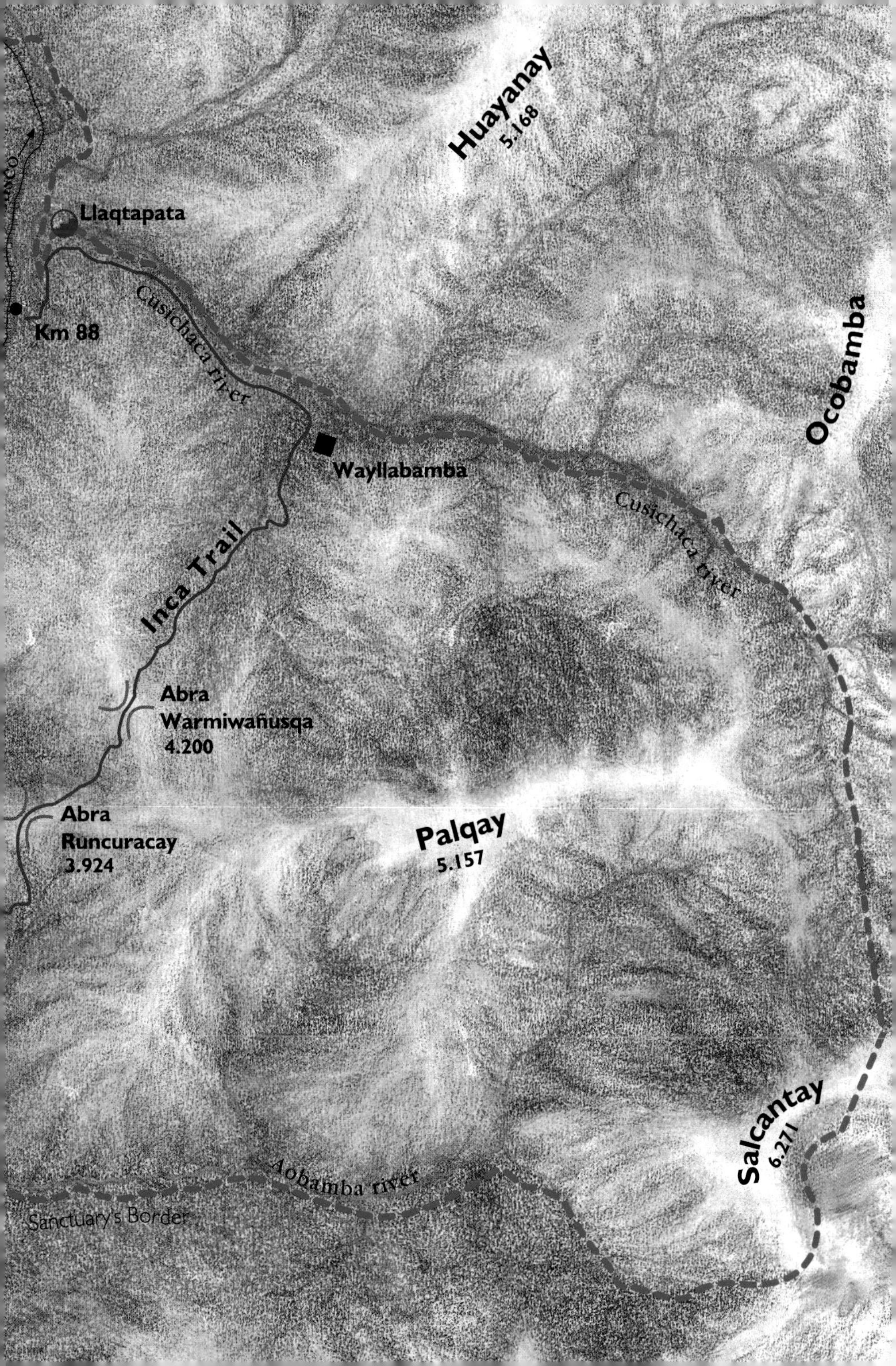
Huayanay
5.168
Llaqtapata
Km 88
Cusichaca river
Ocobamba
Wayllabamba
Cusichaca river
Inca Trail
Abra
Warmiwañusqa
4.200
Abra
Runcuracay
3.924
Palqay
5.157
Salcantay
6.271
Aobamba river
Sanctuary's Border

The Machu Picchu Historical Sanctuary (MPHS)

DUE TO THE ENORMOUS CULTURAL and natural attractions of the Inca citadel and its spectacular surroundings (32,592 hectare), they were declared by the State as a Protected Natural Area in 1981. And in 1983, UNESCO declared the Sanctuary a World Heritage Site.

The MPHS is located on the eastern slopes of the Peruvian Andes, approximately at 13° south and 72° west. The archaeological site stands north west of Cusco, about 112 Kms by railway, amidst an impressive geography of steep mountain ridges separated by narrow valleys and deep ravines. The elevations inside the Protected Area range between 6271 m (snow-peaked Salcantay) and 1725 meters (point at which the Urubamba river exits the Sanctuary). The MPHS is important, besides its archaeological value, because of the scenic landscapes and the variety of ecosystems found within its boundaries. Climate differs considerably according to altitude, from very cold and dry at the higher places, to warm and humid at the bottom of the ravines. Rainfall is more frequent from September through April.

Humid Forest, bellow 2.500 m

Puna Grassland, over 3.800 m

Biodiversity in the MPHS

THE EASTERN FORELANDS OF THE TROPICAL ANDES are regarded as one of the world's most biologically diverse areas. So much so, that just within the MPHS, may be represented a good 10% of the whole country's biodiversity.

For just a few instances: more than 200 species of orchids, some 700 species of butterflies and more than 400 species of birds have been recorded inside the Sanctuary's boundaries. To get a better picture of the biological riches of this area, we should compare its bird life figures with any other area around the planet; out of the 9000 world's known bird species, Europe and North America together account for some 1400 species, whereas only in Peru there are nearly 1800 registered.

The MPHS owes its biodiversity to a combination of factors: a great variety of ecosystems generated by a wide altitude range (4546 metres span) which makes possible a good scope of temperatures;

additionally, the high mountain ridges that create microclimates favourable to the evolution of certain species and subspecies, and finally, thanks to the ever present rainfall of the Amazon Basin and the mist that creeps up the sheltered valleys, providing enough humidity the whole year round.

Andean valley, over 2.500 m.

Birds Associated with Fresh Water

1

Neotropic Cormorant

(Phalacrocorax brasilianus)

Other names: Olivaceous Cormorant, Patillo, Cormorán, Cushuri, Cuervo de Mar. **Family:** Phalacrocoracidae - Cormorants. **Habitat:** Freshwater lakes and rivers; estuaries and saline marshes. **Range**: From s USA to all Central and South America. From sea level to 4200 m.

Behavior: It is a diving bird. Catches fish chasing them under water; it also feeds on shellfish and small amphibians. It can be seen flying low over the water surface, alone, in pairs or in groups. Spends a lot of time sitting on dead snags or perched on high spots with its wings and tail held spread to dry. Nests in colonies on trees, bushes or on the ground. It is the only cormorant known to live away from the seashore. Adults are usually all black. It can be seen upstream in the Urubamba River. **64 - 71 cm**

(Merganetta armata)

Other names: Pato de los Torrentes. **Family:** Anatidae - Ducks, Geese.
Habitat: Clear streams and rivers with rushing torrents, in canyons or gorges.
Range: Andes from Venezuela to Argentina and s Chile. From 1000 to 4000 m.

Behavior: Usually found in pairs or family groups. Can be seen sitting upright on rocks and boulders or swimming in fast-flowing turbulent water. It has the ability to dive and swims up the rapid white waters. Escapes danger by diving or swimming downstream. It is the only duck in the world with such behavior and the only one able to live in this difficult habitat. Eats mostly stonefly larvae. Strongly bonded pairs, they both defend their stretch of the river. The female incubates alone. Nests in holes or dense vegetation. Can be seen along the Urubamba River, especially around the town of Aguas Calientes. **36 - 41 cm**

Fasciated Tiger-Heron

(Tigrisoma fasciatum)

Other names: Pumagarza **Family:** Ardeidae - Herons, Egrets.
Habitat: Creeks, fast-flowing rivers and streams; in humid areas and semiarid valleys. **Range:** From Costa Rica to nw Argentina and se Brazil. From 600 to 3300 m.

Behavior: This shy and reclusive heron is found alone or in pairs, perched on rocks and boulders at the edge of turbulent streams, or under the shadows of overhanging plants. Sometimes it remains motionless, the neck fully extent. Is wary and nervous, flushing easily when it perceives danger. Feeds on fish and small prey from near the water. Both male and female hatch and feed the fledglings. Nests are platforms built with twigs or reeds. They retrieve their long necks when they are flying. Can be seen along the Urubamba River near the town of Aguas Calientes, as well as downstream from it. **65 cm**

16

(Plegadis ridgwayi)

Other names: Yanavico. **Family:** Threskiornithidae - Ibises, Spoonbills. **Habitat:** Lakes, rivers, reed beds, marshy areas, muddy creeks, flooded grasslands and wet meadows. **Range:** High Andes of central Peru to n Argentina and Chile. Common between 3500 and 4800 m, but often comes down to sea level.

Behavior: Very sociable bird. Normally seen in flocks of half a dozen to over a hundred individuals where birds actively peck and probe the ground in search of frogs, snails, shellfish, etc. Obtains its food by probing its long bill into mud and shallow water, relying more on touch sensitivity than on sight. Feeds unperturbed. Flies with

extended neck in long wavering lines, often low over the ground. Nests in colonies on tall reeds. Both parents hatch and feed their chicks. In some places, people eat their eggs. Puna Ibises can be seen near Cusco City or along the meadows and grasslands that surround the first stretches of the railway to Machu-Picchu. **56 - 60 cm**

(Larus serranus)

Other names: Gaviota andina, Tiulla. **Family:** Laridae - Gulls.
Habitat: High Andean plains, puna lakes, marshes; also rivers and agricultural fields.
Range: Andes, from Ecuador to central Chile. Common between 2000 and 5000 m.
It can be seen at sea level too.

Behavior: It is the only gull that breeds in the highlands. It is a skilled flyer and swimmer; it does not dive but can submerge to catch small fish or shellfish. It also feeds on insects over grassland and preys on eggs and bird-chicks. They often look for food at dumpsters and landfills. Quite social, nests in colonies on reed marshes or on islands in old coot nests, or builds a floating nest. Both parents feed their chicks and keep intruders away from the nest. In some places people eats their eggs. Can be seen along the Urubamba River or at higher elevations. It can also be found overflying cultivated fields near Cusco and along the meadows and grasslands by the railway to Machu Picchu. **45 cm**

White-capped Dipper

(Cinclus leucocephalus)

Other names: Mirlo Acuático. **Family:** Cinclidae - Dippers. **Habitat:** Rushing mountain streams and rivers with boulders, both in forested and open areas; sometimes small rivulets. **Range:** Andes, from Venezuela to Bolivia. Mostly from 1000 to 3400 m.

Behavior: Small, chunky bird adapted to live in cold and rocky streams. It is very territorial. Usually found in pairs, they can be seen perched upon the rocks, in the middle of a rushing torrent or in the shoreline. Often flicks wings. Catches insects and shellfish among the rocks and boulders in currents. It does not dive as often as other members of the genus. It is a fast flyer, low over the water with quick wing beats. Builds a dome shaped nest in streamside crevices, often underneath a waterfall. Can be seen in most freshwater streams in the Sanctuary, as well as from the train between Ollantaytambo and Machu Picchu. **15 cm**

Bar-winged Cinclodes

(Cinclodes fuscus)

Other names: Churrete. **Family:** Furnariidae - Ovenbirds. **Habitat:** Open puna grasslands near marshes; along lakeshores and streams; also farmland and bushy country. **Range:** Andes from Venezuela to Tierra del Fuego. From 2500 m to snow line. **Similar species:** C. atacamensis.

Behavior: Very common terrestrial bird. Seen alone or in pairs. Highly territorial, usually seen chasing each other. Forages while walking confident on the ground. Eats insects and other invertebrates. Flies swiftly across open ground or along the watercourses. Sings one of the most familiar songs of the high Andes, usually perched upon a rock. During display raises one wing for one or two seconds. They are monogamous and both sexes build the nest and care for the fledglings. Nests in a hole or burrow usually placed in a bank or in an old wall. A common bird in the MPHS's highlands.

16 - 18 cm

(Sayornis nigricans)

Other names: Papamosca del Rio. **Family:** Tyrannidae - Flycatchers. **Habitat:** Near rocky streams in mountains, often with overhanging vegetation; also parks, but never far from the water. **Range:** Andes from Venezuela to Bolivia and n Argentina. From 500 to 2800 m.

Behavior: A tame, confiding, active and familiar bird often seen perched on a rock in the middle of swift moving rivers. Occurs alone or in pairs. Sallies short distances above the surface to catch insects, returning to the same perch. Frequently wags tail. Nests near the water, on a rocky ledge, on crevices or under a bridge. Common along the Urubamba River and its tributaries. **15 - 17 cm**

Torrent Tyrannulet

(Serpophaga cinerea)

Other names: Cazamoscas del Torrente. **Family:** Tyrannidae - Flycatchers.
Habitat: Both humid and arid zones; fast-flowing rocky rivers and streams; also flooded forests. **Range:** From Costa Rica south through the Andes to Bolivia. From 700 to 2800 m.

Behavior: Spritely and alert, a bird of rushing torrents. Can be seen perched on rocks and boulders along the rivers or upon branches overhanging the water, usually in pairs. Sallies to surface of rocks or to vegetation along riverbank for flying insects. It also runs to pick up prey from the gravel or even from the water. Occasionally adventures further away from the water to forage in grassland. It likes nesting in branches overhanging water. Often flicks tail upward. Commonly seen along the Urubamba River and its tributaries.

II cm

Raptors or Carrion-eaters

2

Roadside Hawk

(Buteo magnirostris)

Other names: Aguilucho, Gavilán, Micmichu, Arriero. **Family:** Accipitridae - Hawks, Eagles. **Habitat:** Humid lowland and forests; bushy country, clearings, forest edges. **Range:** Mexico to n Argentina and Brazil. Common in the lowlands, occasionally ascends to 3000 m on e Andean slopes. **Similar species:** Buteo spp.

Behavior: A diurnal sluggish bird of prey. Its flight is weak, alternating a quick flapping with a glide, and seldom does it far. Soars sporadically. Its ability to search for prey in the foliage makes up for its flying limitations. Eats insects, snakes and other vertebrates. Nests in trees. Like all hawks it has strong bill and claws, the female is larger than the male, its population density is low, and their territories are vast. The name "Roadside hawk" originates in rural areas, where it is frequently seen beside the roads. In wilder country, where there are no roads, this bird prefers the edge of rivers. It can be seen in flight or perched on branches and snags along the river near the town of Aguas Calientes. **33 - 40 cm**

(Geranoaetus melanoleucus)

Other names: Aguilucho Grande.
Family: Accipitridae - Hawks,
Eagles. **Habitat:** Semiarid and
open country, sparsely wooded
country, valleys and rocky open
slopes; occurs rarely in the
higher puna grasslands.
Range: Andes from
Venezuela to Tierra del Fuego,
including s Brazil and n
Argentina. Up to 3800 m.

Behavior: A large chunky diurnal
raptor with strong hooked bill and
gripping feet. Female is bigger than
male. Alone or in pairs, they stand on
rocks, on the ground and sometimes upon
tree branches. More likely to be seen soaring
high gracefully over ridges. Same as all eagles, its
population density is low and their territories are
vast. Eats anything available:
snakes, rodents, small birds and
even carrion. Their twig nests are
built on rock ledges or cliffs.
Farmers hunt them because they
often prey on their chickens.
Common in the Inca Trail. **61 - 80 cm**

(Falco femoralis)

Other names: Halcón Perdiguero. **Family:** Falconidae - Falcons, Caracaras. **Habitat:** Dry to arid areas with scattered trees, grasslands, scrubs, rugged mountain, Eucalyptus groves. **Range:** From the south of North America to Tierra del Fuego. From 2000 to 4600 m; some times descends to the coast. **Similar species:** F. peregrinus.

Behavior: Long-tailed and streamlined bird. Occurs usually alone. Perches on small trees, from where it scans for insects, small birds, mice and bats. Flies swiftly and fast with elegant turns; often hovers, seldom soars. It hunts flying low and, like all falcons, is very fast when it stoops over its prey. Sometimes seeks food following the grassland burnings. They don't build their own nests but use the ones left by other birds, or settle directly on suitable holes in the rocks. Falcons are omnivorous and opportunistic, if need be, scavengers. Some people train them for hunting. Can be seen in the dry higher grounds of the MPHS. **36 - 46 cm**

(Falco sparverius)

Other names: Cernícalo, Quilli-quilli, Quillicha. **Family:** Falconidae - Falcons, Caracaras. **Habitat:** Forest edges, dry areas, open country with scattered trees or rocky outcrops, including villages; avoids densely forested areas. **Range:** All over North and South America, except for thick tropical forests. From sea level to 4500 m.

Behavior: A small hawk, less powerful than other falcons. Often quite self-confident. It occurs alone or in pairs. The female is slightly larger than male. When perched, frequently bobs tail up and down. It searches for prey soaring up in the air or perching alert on a branch or rock, then stoop down on them. It normally eats insects, but it can also eat snakes and rodents. It breeds in rock-ledges or in cavities in trees, termite nests or derelict empty houses. It is quite common in the MPHS. **23 - 28 cm**

Andean Condor

(Vultur gryphus)

Other names: Condor. **Family:** Cathartidae - American Vultures. **Habitat:** High, steep mountains and canyons in desolate areas; roosts in rocky cliffs.
Range: Throughout the Andes from Venezuela to Tierra del Fuego. Common between 2000 and 5200 m, but often descends to sea level.
Similar species: Cathartes aura.

Behavior: It can be found alone, in pairs or larger groups. Feeds on carrion (occasionally on garbage). It can travel hundreds of kilometres, and spend hours gliding majestically along canyon walls or ,aring high above the hillsides, seeking a carcass to feed on. They have difficulties to take off after meals, due to the excessive weight. It nests in inaccessible rocky cliffs. The young take six years to fully develop. Often stands with spread wings. Together with the Californian Condor, they are the world's biggest flying animals. The Condor was much revered by pre-Hispanic civilizations, and up to present day, it still plays an important role in many cultural manifestations of the Andean peoples. On occasions, it can be seen around the Machu Picchu ruins but it is more likely to be found at the higher reaches of the Inca Trail. **100 - 130 cm; wingspan = 300 cm**

Mountain Caracara

(Phalcoboenus megalopterus)

Other names: Chinalinda **Family:** Falconidae - Falcons, Caracaras.
Habitat: Open puna grasslands, high mountains, plowed land. **Range:** Heights of Peru,
n Argentina and n Chile. From 3000 to 5000 m.

Behavior: Unmistakable diurnal predator of long wings and tail.
They are omnivorous and opportunistic, even scavengers.
It feeds on the ground in open plains and grazed
areas, where it is usual to see them walking in
pairs or groups, searching for insects. At times,
there can be hundreds in plowed fields. It
nests on rock ledges. Roosts in groups in cliffs.
Easily seen around the Inca Trail as well as
along the higher section of the railway to
Macchu Picchu. **53 cm**

Birds of Open Areas and Agricultural Fields

3

Andean Flicker

(Colaptes rupicola)

Other names: Pito, Gargacha. **Family:** Picidae - Woodpeckers. **Habitat:** Puna grasslands, fields and scrub of high Andes. Avoids wooded areas. **Range:** Peru to n Argentina and n Chile. From 2000 to 5000 m.

Behavior: A striking, mainly terrestrial woodpecker with a very long bill. Wary but easy to watch. Like all woodpeckers it has a strong bill and a long, barbed tongue that extends enabling it to reach bark and wood boring insects. Spends much time on the ground. Gregarious and loose flocks move across open country, amongst the rocks and scattered trees, probing for ants and other insects into crevices and cracks or digging into the ground with their beaks. Display consists of rising up the bills and flicking the wings. Nests in holes excavated in banks and old walls. It is said to be useful in natural medicine practices and it has a place in ancient local mythology. Commonly found in the higher spots along the Inca Trail.

30 - 35 cm

(Carduelis magellanica)

Other names: Jilguero. **Family:** Fringillidae - Siskins. **Habitat:** Humid and semiarid shrubbery, forest edges, semi open or cultivated areas with scattered trees, parks and gardens. Avoids dense forests. **Range:** Andes from Colombia to n Chile; Venezuela and Guyana; the River Plate basin region. From lowlands to 5000 m.
Similar species: C. crassirostris.

Behavior: Very gregarious, often quite tame bird with a distinctive bounding fly. Feeds in trees and shrubbery, sometimes at the ground. It has a short beak, adapted to eating hard seeds. Often seen in pairs or small groups, foraging at all levels of vegetation, sometimes in mixed flocks. Appreciated as an ornamental bird, due to its colours and pleasant singing. Very common in the Inca Trail, around Llactapata ruins and along the railway to Machu Picchu.

II - I2 cm

(Catamenia analis)

Other names: Corbatita. **Family:** Emberizinae - Finches. **Habitat:** Both dry and humid areas; grasslands and scrubs, agricultural areas, gardens, pastures, hedgerows. **Range:** Andes of Colombia to n Chile and nw Argentina. From 1000 to 3700 m, and lower on Peruvian Pacific slope. **Similar species:** C. homochroa.

Behavior: A bird with a heavy conical bill adapted to feed on seeds. It has a rather loud but attractive song. It can be seen foraging seeds in the shrubs or at ground level, in pairs or small groups; often joins in mixed flocks with other finches. It has an undulating flight. Common in the Inca Trail and in the shrubbery along the railway tracks. **11 - 12 cm**

(Phrygilus plebejus)

Other names: Plomito. **Family:** Emberizinae - Finches. **Habitat:** Grassy and shrubby areas, sparsely vegetated stony areas; also bushy ravines and cactus-covered slopes.
Range: Andes of n Chile and nw Argentina. From 2400 to 4500 m.
Similar species: P. unicolor.

Behavior: One of the most conspicuous and numerous birds in the high Andes. It is terrestrial: forages on the ground and perches over the bushes, rocks or cactuses. It feeds on seeds. Usually occurs in pairs or groups, often in large mixed finch flocks. Roosts in the bushes and flies to open country during the day. Almost all species of Phrygilus live very high in the Andes, hence the name "Sierra Finches". It is easy to find and watch along the Inca Trail. **l2 cm**

Bright-rumped Yellow-Finch

(Sicalis uropygialis)

Other names: Chirigüe, Trile Altoandino. **Family:** Emberizinae - Finches. **Habitat:** High puna grassland, often on rocky slopes interspersed with grass and open ground; arid scrub; around farms with stonewalls. **Range:** Andes of Peru to nw Argentina. From 3300 to 4800 m. **Similar species:** S. olivascens.

Behavior: Common in the high puna. Usually found in flocks, sometimes of up to 500 individuals. It often occurs near watercourses and associated to other species. Like most Emberizinae finch, its beak is heavy and conical, adapted to break open hard seeds. It forages for seeds on the ground. Breeds and roosts in cliffs, holes in banks, stone fences, burrows in the ground or under roofing eaves. It can be seen near the houses in Cusco city, along the railway tracks to Machu Picchu, and along the higher sections of the Inca Trail. **13 - 14 cm**

(Zonotrichia capensis)

Other names: Gorrión Americano, Pichizanka. **Family:** Emberizinae - Finches.
Habitat: Open or semiopen areas; arid scrub, humid shrubby areas, agricultural fields, parks and gardens in towns. **Range:** From Mexico to most of South America, except in the Amazone basin. From sea level to 5000 m.

Behavior: A widespread, abundant and very common Andean bird. Tame and confiding, it can be seen foraging on the ground for seeds and insects, or perched on bushes or hedgerows. They are often numerous in parks and lawns in towns. Their nests are neat cups on the ground. Like many Emberizinae finches, its song is attractive and can be heard usually after a rain-shower and occasionally at night. It can be watched hopping around the Inca walls at the Machu Picchu ruins. **14 - 15 cm**

Birds of Shrubby Areas, Lighter Woodland or Forest Edges

4

(Synallaxis azarae)

Other names: Coliespina. **Family:** Furnariidae - Ovenbirds. **Habitat:** Always in dense vegetation in humid forests, shrubby forest borders, overgrown clearings, bamboo thickets and roadsides. **Range:** Andes of w Venezuela to nw Argentina. From 1500 to 3500 m; lower at the south end of its range.

Behavior: A furtive bird very common in the Andes. More likely to be heard than seen, for its call keeps ringing continuously throughout the day. It creeps and hops actively inside dense shrubbery, grass or tangles, nearly always close to the ground, although at times it perches in the open for a few seconds. Occurs in pairs or family groups. Like other Ovenbirds they are monogamous. Both parents build their basket-like nests and take care of the fledglings. It can be found along the railway tracks between Aguas Calientes and Puente Ruinas.

17 - 18 cm

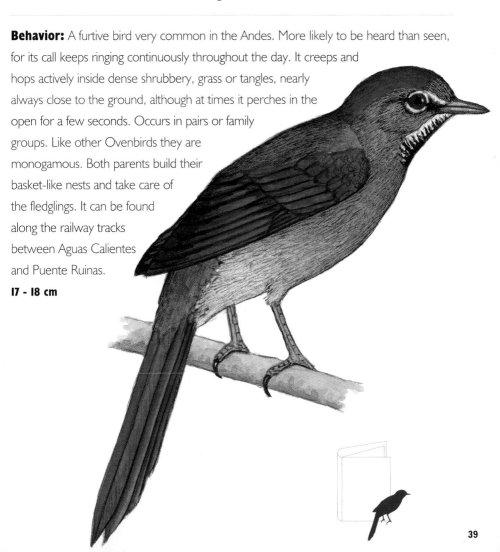

(Anairetes parulus)

Other names: Torito. **Family:** Tyrannidae - Flycatchers. **Habitat:** Both humid and arid areas; stunted forest borders, shrubbery, semi open bushy hillsides, semiarid isolated forest patches, Polylepis forests. **Range:** Andes of s Colombia to Tierra del Fuego. From 1800 to 4200 m. **Similar species:** A. flavirostris.

Behavior: Very restless and aggressive birds, they are often chasing one another. Found in pairs or family groups foraging rather low in dense bushes and trees. Seldom found in mixed species flocks. It perches and hover-gleans among twigs, leaves and flowers, and makes short aerial sallies for insects. It frequently pivots on the perch. It shivers the wings nervously and flicks the tail. Its nest is a small cup in shrubs or bamboo. Fairly common at Machu Picchu between 2500 and 3600 m.

10 - 11 cm

(Cyanocorax yncas)

Other names: Quién quién. **Family:** Corvidae - Jays. **Habitat:** Dry and humid forests; forest edges and borders, lighter woodland, trees and shrubbery in clearings, plantations; tolerates habitats altered by man. **Range:** S Texas to Venezuela and Andes to n Bolivia. From 1300 to 2700 m.

Behavior: A robust, active and noisy perching bird. Gregarious, it occurs in groups, foraging at all levels of the forest, on permanent territories. Opportunistic and omnivorous, it is daring and curious at times. Very sociable, they keep in family groups all year round and nest in a cooperative way. The immature help the parents with the care of the nestlings. The nest is a shallow, loosely woven basket high in the tree. Very vocal bird, with a variety of loud calls. It is unmistakable and can be seen along the railway tracks between Puente Ruinas and the Mandor Valley. **29 - 32 cm**

Chiguanco Thrush

(Turdus chiguanco)

saw april 3rd by on walk by urubamba River

Other names: Chiguanco. **Family:** Turdidae - Thrushes. **Habitat:** Open country in semiarid habitats, but usually near water; scrubby woodland with cactus, shrubbery areas, agricultural fields with scattered trees, hedgerows, gardens. **Range:** S Ecuador to nw Argentina. From 2000 to 4000 m and lower in the Peruvian Coast.

Similar species: T. serranus, T. fuscater.

Behavior: It is very common and numerous in the high Andes. Often quite tame. It happens alone or in pairs, running and hopping about in garden grounds, searching for prey and flicking the tail. Eats fruit and frequents the fields in groups. It builds substantial cup nests. Like all Trushes it sings a variety of beautiful songs, but only in the breeding season. The species of the genus Turdus are considered among the finest songbird species in the world. Look up for it around the Llactapata ruins in the Inca Trail. **28 cm**

(Troglodytes aedon)

Other names: Cucarachero, Turriche. **Family:** Troglodytidae - Wrens.
Habitat: All open or semi open habitats in humid or arid regions; puna grassland, scrub, shrubbery, gardens, farmyards, forest edges; avoids dense forests. **Range:** Throughout the American continent from Canada to Tierra del Fuego. From sea level to 4000 m.
Similar species: T. solstitialis.

Behavior: Abundant and widespread cheerful bird. Confident and curious, it is a virtual commensal of man. More numerous near human settlements than in wild zones. Active, nervous and often tame, it cocks its tail when it searches for insects, creeping and skulking amid the twigs or on the ground. It is easier to hear it than to see it. It builds its nests in holes on the walls, shrubbery or even the ground. It is quite common around peopled areas. It can be seen in the village of Aguas Calientes. **11 - 12 cm**

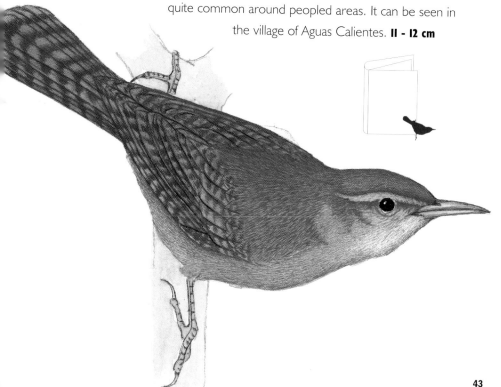

43

Bananaquit

(Coereba flaveola)

Other names: Mielero, Reinita, Bananero. **Family:** Coerebinae - Conebill.
Habitat: Semi-open to open habitats in both humid and arid regions; forest edges, thorny woodland and scrub, lighter woodland and shrubbery, plantations, gardens.
Range: Mexico to Norwest Argentina and Brazil. Omnipresent on West Indies. Mostly below 1500 m, reaches 2400 m in the MPHS.

Behaviour: Energetic, restless bird of melodic singing with a short, curved bill. It is the only species of its family. It moves alone, in pairs or in family groups through trees and bushes at any level, sucking the flowers' nectar or searching for insects and fruit. Sometimes is so tame that it can sip from the sugar bowls at houses and hotels. Their nests are oval-shaped, untidy balls. It also builds structures called "dummies" or "dormitory nests". It sings from high branches. Look out for it along the river, between Aguas Calientes and Puente Ruinas. **10 - 11 cm**

(Conirostrum cinereum)

Other names: Mielerito gris **Family:** Thraupinae - Tanagers. **Habitat:** Both in humid and arids regions; forest borders, scrub and schrubbery, fields with scattered shrubs, Polylepis forests, hedgerows, gardens; avoid forested areas. **Range:** Andes of sw Colombia to n Chile and western Bolivia. From the Pacific coast to 4500 m.

Behavoir: Active, nervous bird with a sharply pointed bill. It occurs alone, in pairs or small family groups. It looks for insects and berries hopping among the bushes. Spends most of its time moving along middle branches inside vegetation. It perches and sings from the centre of its territory. Like all Tanagers, it forms mixed species flocks. The nests are cups of woven fibre, built on trees. It can be seen near the Llactapata ruins at the Inca Trail. **II - I2 cm**

(Diglossa brunneiventris)

Other names: Robaflor. **Family:** Thraupinae - Tanagers. **Habitat:** Mainly dry areas; scrub and shrubby areas, forest borders, Polylepis forests, gardens and agricultural areas. **Range:** Andes of n Colombia; Perú to n Chile. From 2000 to 4000 m. **Similar species:** D. sittoides.

Behavior: This bird have an upturned, slightly hooked bill specialized for piercing the base of flowers. Very active, it constantly moves at lower and mid strata of vegetation, piercing flowers for nectar. It can be seen hanging upside down from branches, searching for insects. It is an aggressive defender of its feeding area from intruders like hummingbirds, conebills and other flower-piercers. Makes courtship flights. Like many Tanagers, takes part in mixed flocks. Its nest is a deep cup of grass and moss atop a tree. It can be seen along the Inca Trail. **13 - 15 cm**

(Pipraeidea melanonota)

Other names: Chachaquito, Viuva. **Family:** Thraupinae - Tanagers.

Habitat: Semi open areas; forest edge and borders, lighter woodland, overgrown pastures, clearings with scattered trees, cultivated areas, gardens; absent mostly from forested regions. **Range:** Andes from Venezuela to Bolivia; ne Argentina and southeastern Brazil. From 1400 to 3000 m; lower at se South America.

Similar species: Delothraupis castaneoventris.

Behavior: Easily recognized bird. Alone or in pairs, it may perch at virtually any level. Gleans for fruits and insects in trees and bushes, frequently hanging, and sallies for flying insects. It travels over wide areas in search of food. Not a sociable bird. Unlike other Tanagers, it never joins mixed flocks, but can join feeding aggregation at fruiting trees. You can find it near the Puente Ruinas bridge.

14 - 15 cm

(Piranga flava)

Other names: Frutero. **Family:** Thraupinae - Tanagers. **Habitat:** Forests and scrub both in humid and arid areas; open woodland, forest borders, clearings, plantations. **Range:** Andes from Venezuela to Bolivia; n coast of Peru; n of Brazil and the Guyana; se Brazil and ne Argentina; sw USA to Panama. From 1500 to 3000 m. **Similar species:** P. rubra.

Behavior: A sluggish, arboreal bird. It happens alone or in pairs, moving rather slowly at all levels of the vegetation, but mainly in the higher parts of the trees. It peers deliberately at foliage, twigs and branches. Very rarely seen in flocks. The nests are frail and flat, sometimes rather low on a tree. It can be found along the railway tracks between Puente Ruinas and the Mandor Valley. **17 - 19 cm**

(Ramphocelus carbo)

Other names: Pico plata. **Family:** Thraupinae - Tanagers. **Habitat:** Shrubby and edge habitats; clearings, gardens, forest borders. **Range:** All Amazon basin including parts of Venezuela, Guyana and Paraguay. Up to 2000 m or more in the Andes.

Behavior: Like other species of Ramphocelus, it has a characteristic metallic-silver mandible. It moves fast, in noisy pairs or groups, around the undergrowth and shrubbery, searching for fruits and insects. It is more likely to be found in places near the water. It seldom forms mixed species flocks. It can be seen near the town of Aguas Calientes. **16 - 18 cm**

(Tangara cyanicollis)

Other names: Tangara Rey. **Family:** Thraupinae - Tanagers. **Habitat:** Semiopen humid habitats with trees and shrubbery, bushy pastures, forest edges, cultivated areas, gardens; never inside the forest. **Range:** Andes from Venezuela to Bolivia and w Amazonian Brazil. From 500 to 2400 m.

Behavior: It is mostly frugivorous. Lazes about atop the trees or sallies clumsily to air or hops in the foliage, then flies to a fruiting tree. It hangs from leaves for berries and inspects branches, limbs and flower heads. It sallies for insects too. Occurs usually in pairs or small groups and forages independently from mixed flocks. Its nests are open cups placed on trees. It is common around the town of Aguas Calientes. **13 cm**

(Saltator aurantiirostris)

Other names: Pipitero, Pepitero. **Family:** Cardinalinae - Grosbeaks, Saltators.
Habitat: Both humid and dry regions; scrubs, shrubbery, forest edges, hedgerows, gardens, Eucalyptus trees. **Range:** Highlands of Peru and Bolivia; n Argentina, w Paraguay and Uruguay. To at least 3700 m.

Behavior: Shy and jittery bird. It sings well hidden in the upper foliage of trees and bushes, but feeds at ground level where it forages for insects, seeds and berries. Like other Cardinalinae species, it moves mostly in pairs, but sometimes also in family groups. It is fairly common around the Wayllabamba Village in the Inca Trail. **19 - 20 cm**

(Pheucticus aureoventris)

Other names: Pipitero, Pepitero. **Family:** Cardinalinae - Grosbeaks, Saltators. **Habitat:** Cloud forests, humid forests and adjacent semiarid zones; semi open areas with scattered trees, shrubby areas, wooded ravines, streams with alder trees (Alnus sp), cultivated areas with hedgerows, corn fields, gardens. **Range:** Andes from Venezuela to Bolivia and arid lowlands to nw Argentina. Up to 3700 m.

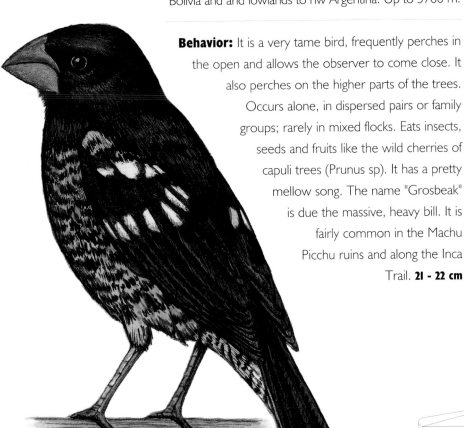

Behavior: It is a very tame bird, frequently perches in the open and allows the observer to come close. It also perches on the higher parts of the trees. Occurs alone, in dispersed pairs or family groups; rarely in mixed flocks. Eats insects, seeds and fruits like the wild cherries of capuli trees (Prunus sp). It has a pretty mellow song. The name "Grosbeak" is due the massive, heavy bill. It is fairly common in the Machu Picchu ruins and along the Inca Trail. **21 - 22 cm**

(Pheucticus chrysogaster)

Other names: Southern Yellow Grosbeak, Yellow Grosbeak, Pipitero, Pepitero. **Family:** Cardinalinae - Grosbeaks, Saltators. **Habitat:** Both humid and semiarid regions; forest borders, bushy slopes, scrub, gardens, hedgerows, cultivated areas with scattered trees, Eucalyptus groves. **Range:** Mountains of n Venezuela, Andes from Ecuador to s Peru. From 1500 to 3500 m.

Behavior: Similar to Black-backed Grosbeak (Pheucticus aureoventris). It often raids the cornfields. **20 - 21 cm**

Birds in Groups:
Flying or Perched
at Trees

5

(Columba maculosa)

Other names: Paloma cenicienta. **Family:** Columbidae - Pigeons, Doves.
Habitat: Semiarid habitats; open woodland, scrubs, agricultural fields, villages, Eucalyptus trees; avoids humid forests. **Range:** Andes of s Peru down to central Argentina and s Brazil. From 2000 to 4000 m. **Similar species:** C. plumbea.

Behavior: A social, large pigeon. It perches in the canopy on exposed branches, but it feeds on the ground; it likes eating seeds. Found in small groups or breeding pairs, but sometimes in large flocks. In ground display, fans and raises tail and holds wings somewhat out. It breeds and roosts in trees. Like all Columbidae species, the chicks are fed "pigeon milk" by regurgitation. Look up for it around the Llactapata ruins in the Inca Trail. **33 cm**

(Metriopelia ceciliae)

Other names: Cascabelita, Tortolita. **Family:** Columbidae - Pigeons, Doves **Habitat:** Arid and temperate zones; open rocky and sandy places with cactus and herbaceous plants, lightly wooded areas, and around human habitation. **Range:** Andes of Peru to n Chile and nw Argentina. From 2500 to 4500 m.

Behavior: It is a silent bird, never heard singing. It may be watched searching for seeds on the ground, usually in small groups. Often takes dust-bathes. When it flushes, it generally flies a short distance to a near branch, a cliff face or a rock. Their wings produce a buzz like sound when they fly. Nests in holes in the ground, cliff faces or in the walls and roofs of rural buildings. Appropriately to Columbidae species, the chicks are fed "pigeon milk" by regurgitation. Can be found near the Llactapata ruins in the Inca Trail. **19 cm**

(Zenaida auriculata)

Other names: Rabiblanca, Madrugadora. **Family:** Columbidae - Pigeons, Doves.
Habitat: Semi-arid open areas and cultivated fields with scattered trees and bushes.
Range: All over South America. From 600 to 4000 m
Similar species: Leptotila verreauxi.

Behavior: It is a gregarious, sociable bird. Roosts and nests in communities, in trees or rocks, on flimsy stick platforms, but feeds at ground level. Flies swiftly, fast and directly, without sailings. Large flocks often gather to feed at cultivated fields, causing considerable losses to farmers. Due to this fact and their numerous population, they are sought after by hunters. As all Columbidae, the chicks are fed by regurgitation. It can be seen around Wayllabamba Village in the Inca Trail. **23 - 28 cm**

(Aratinga mitrata)

Other names: Cotorra.
Family: Psittacidae - Parrots.
Habitat: Mostly in humid forests with plenty of rocky cliffs.
Range: From central Andes of Peru to nw Argentina. Mostly from 1800 to 2500 m. and sometimes higher. **Similar species:** A. wagleri, Leptosittaca branickii.

Behavior: Very sociable, noisy and gregarious birds. They can be seen in large, noisy flocks feeding in the canopy, often in flowering pisonay trees (Erythrina sp). They also invade cultivated land and farmers treat them as a plague. They eat fruits, seeds, buds, flowers and even clay. As it happens with all parrots, mating pairs are for life. They nest in cliff holes and hollow trees. The female cares for the young and the male feeds them by regurgitation. It can be seen around Aguas Calientes, in the Urubamba gorge. **38 cm**

(Pionus tumultuosus)

Other names: Loro. **Family:** Psittacidae - Parrots. **Habitat:** Temperate zones, humid forests, forest edges, tall cloud forests with bamboo thickets. **Range:** Andes of w Venezuela to Peru and w Bolivia. From 1400 to 3300 m.
Similar species: P. menstruus, Amazona mercenaria.

Behavior: Highly nomadic bird. Can be seen feeding on the treetops or flying across the valleys in pairs or flocks. Flies with very deep wing beats. Often raids corn fields causing losses to farmers. Eats fruits, seeds and blossoms. Nests in holes in the trees. Appropriately to all parrots, the female cares for the young and the male feeds them by regurgitation. Can be seen in the lower reaches of the Aobamba Valley. **27 - 29 cm**

(Uropsalis lyra)

Other names: Chotacabras. **Family:** Caprimulgidae - Nighthawks, Nightjars. **Habitat:** Openings at edges of humid forests; clearings and glades, nearly always by cliff faces or rocky ravines. **Range:** East slopes of the Andes from w Venezuela to nw Argentina. From 800 to 3500 m. **Similar species:** U. segmentata, Caprimulgus longirostris.

Behavior: The male boasts a tail sometimes three times the size of his body. It has nocturnal habits and its plumage mingles with the environment, therefore, it is easier to hear it than to see it. Becomes visible only when it flushes or at displays at dusk. They spend the day sitting on the ground, camouflaged amongst leaf litter, or they crawl short distances looking for food. They lay their eggs on ledges on cliff faces, usually near the ground. They sally at night from a low perch, less often from the ground, to catch insects in flight. They have a communal display. On courtship, several males may circle and chase females. They can be seen at dusk near the hot springs in Aguas Calientes. **25 - 28 cm, not including the male's tail**

(Notiochelidon cyanoleuca)

Other names: Santa Rosita, Golondrina. **Family:** Hirundinidae - Swallows.
Habitat: Semi open and open country both in humid and arid regions; forest clearings, along rivers; common in towns and agricultural regions. **Range:** Widespread from s Mexico throughout Central and South America, but absent at the core of the Amazon jungle. Up to 3500 m. **Similar species:** N. flavipes.

Behavior: Common, gregarious, migratory bird with slightly forked tail and long pointed wings. It spends a long time in the air, where it is very agile; by contrast, it is rather clumsy on the ground. Flies erratically, relatively high and in large flocks. It catches insects on the wing. Roosts on branches, wires or roofs, usually in the company of other swallows. They nest both ways, as separate pairs or in groups, in eaves, trees, crevices of cliffs or holes in the walls, including old Inca walls. It uses mud to build its nest. Can be seen at the Machu Picchu ruins or in the town of Aguas Calientes.

12 - 13 cm

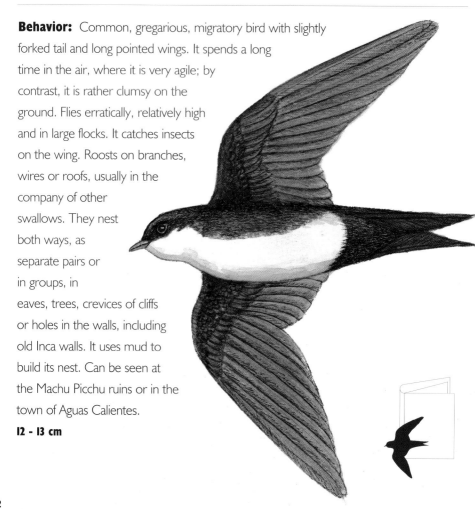

Flycatchers:
Perched or in
Acrobating Flight

6

Smoke-colored Pewee

(Contopus fumigatus)

Other names: Greater Pewee. **Family:** Tyrannidae Flycatchers. **Habitat:** Humid forests; forest borders, clearings with scattered trees, dead branches and fallen trees. **Range:** Costa Rica to Venezuela and Guyana. Andes to nw Argentina. Mostly from 1000 to 3000 m, and lower on Pacific slope. **Similar species:** C. cooperi.

Behavior: A tame bird with a prominent bushy crest. Solitary, except when breeding. Specialized in aerial hawking. Sits erect and alert on an exposed dead snag or branch, not too high, from which it sallies long distances for aerial insects, returning repeatedly to the same perch, shivering the tail when it alights. Their nest is a moss and lichen cup, saddled on a horizontal branch on a tree. Although it will seldom be heard singing, it will be easily found along the railway tracks between Aguas Calientes and the Mandor Valley.

17 cm

(Elaenia albiceps)

Other names: Fiofío. **Family:** Tyrannidae - Flycatchers. **Habitat:** Humid and arid regions; bushy areas, partially wooded terrain, stunted forest borders, edges of clearings, gardens, orchards; likes molle trees (Schinus sp) and willows (Salix sp). **Range:** From Colombia to Tierra del Fuego on both slopes of the Andes and Brazil. Mostly below 3300 m. **Similar species:** E. flavogaster, E. parvirostris.

Behavior: An active but shy bird that perches upright. Found alone or in pairs. Feeds on berries picked by sally gleaning, hover-gleaning or reaching down; it also sallies for flying insects. Its nest is a cup on a small tree. This species is easily mistaken for others of its genus. Is very common at the MPHS.

13 - 15 cm

White-winged Black-Tyrant

(Knipolegus aterrimus)

Other names: Viudita **Family:** Tyrannidae - Flycatchers.**Habitat:** Humid and arid regions; light scrub, forest borders, scrubby slopes, clearings. **Range:** Andes from Peru to Bolivia, from 1500 to 3000 m, and lower at w Paraguay and w Argentina. **Similar species:** K. signatus.

Behavior: Solitary or in pairs perches erectly in the open, generally rather quite, on top of small trees. Sallies into the air, to foliage or to the ground in search of prey. Flicks tail upon landing. Breeding males perform a display flight that traces an arc in mid air with a short jump, followed by the utterance of their song. Nests are open cups built at low level on trees and shrubs. It can be easily found in the Machu Picchu ruins or along the road from the ruins to Aguas Calientes. **16 - 18 cm**

Golden-crowned Flycatcher

(Myiodynastes chrysocephalus)

Other names: Atrapamoscas **Family:** Tyrannidae - Flycatchers.

Habitat: Humid forests; forest borders, riversides, clearings with scattered tall trees.

Range: Panama and Andes from n Venezuela to s Bolivia. From 900 to 2500 m.

Similar species: M. maculatus.

Behavior: Rather noisy bird, with several loud calls. Single or separated pairs often nod as they perch at low to moderate heights on an exposed limb near foliage. It also sits motionless for long periods in upright posture. It hawks for insects and returns to the same perch. Eats fruit as well. Sometimes joins mixed flocks but prefers to remain apart. It nests in crevices or holes in trees. Look up for it along the banks of the Urubamba River between Aguas Calientes and the Mandor Valley. **20 - 2I cm**

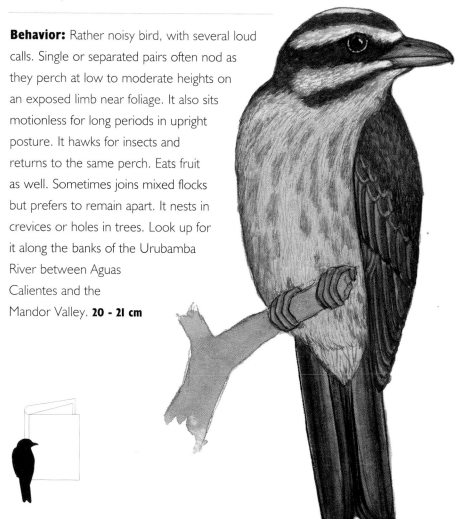

Streak-throated Bush-Tyrant

(Myiotheretes striaticollis)

Other names: Chifla perro. **Family:** Tyrannidae - Flycatchers. **Habitat:** Semi open regions; scrub, open pastures, open wooded ravines, clearings and landslides in forests, farms, hedgerows, gardens, Eucalyptus groves; avoids forested regions. **Range:** Andes from Venezuela to nw Argentina. From 1500 to 3700 m; sometimes lower to 500 m. **Similar species:** M. fuscorufus.

Behavior: A large, tame flycatcher. Always occurs at low densities, single or in pairs. It perches at open high places like rocks or bushes, from where it scans the surroundings to sally long distances, catching insects in swooping aerial forays. Also jumps to the ground for prey and then flies back to the same perch. Very common in the Sanctuary, it can be seen in the Machu Picchu ruins. **21 - 23 cm**

Possibly hooded siskin

(Myiozetetes similis)

Other names: Vermilion-crowned Flycatcher, Atrapamoscas. **Family:** Tyrannidae - Flycatchers. **Habitat:** Shrubby clearings, canopy and borders of forests and lighter woodland, agricultural fields, gardens and residential areas. **Range:** Mexico to Panama. E slopes of the Andes to all Amazon basin, including Venezuela and se Brazil. Mostly below 1000 m, reaches the 2000 m in the MPHS.

Behavior: An active, excitable and noisy bird, often drawing attention by its varying, loud calls. Found in pairs or family groups on exposed perches at all levels, from ground to tree tops. Very fond of gathering around fruiting trees to take berries in quick hovers. Often drops down to ground for prey. Nests are untidy ball-like made of grass, often over water or near bee or ant nests. Look up for it along the railway tracks between Puente Ruinas and the Mandor Valley. **16 - 17 cm**

was a Territipamid no ? apt74
by land on Trunk

White-browed Chat-Tyrant

(Ochthoeca leucophrys)

Other names: Pitajo. **Family:** Tyrannidae - Flycatchers. **Habitat:** Mostly in quite arid regions; shrubby areas, patches of woodland, xerophytic scrub, ravines, gorges, farms, hedgerows; often near water; avoids humid forests. **Range:** Andes of Peru to nw Argentina. From 2000 to 3500 m; lower in some places. **Similar species:** O. fumicolor, O. oenanthoides.

Behavior: An attractive, chunky shaped bird. Alone or in pairs which typically take prominent perches, often atop a bush or low tree. It perches erectly, frequently jerking wings and tail. Catches insects on the ground or in mid air and flies back to the same perch. Differently from other Andean Tyrants, it does not join in mixed flocks. Easy to watch along the Inca Trail. **15 cm**

(Pyrrhomyias cinnamomea)

Other names: Atrapamoscas. **Family:** Tyrannidae - Flycatchers. **Habitat:** Humid shrubby forest borders, forest clearings, along tracks and trails, stunted forests with admixed bamboo. **Range:** N Venezuela and the Andes from Colombia to nw Argentina. Mostly from 1200 to 3300 m; lower in some places.

Behavior: A conspicuous, attractive and remarkably tame bird. It is highly sedentary; seldom leaving its same restricted area. Occurs in pairs and does not follow any mixed flock. Perches erect and alert atop a bush or small tree. Sallies for insects short distances, to air or foliage, and then return to the same perch. Nests on rock ledges, fallen logs or crevices in rocks or barks. This tame bird is easy to watch along the roads and railway tracks near Aguas Calientes. **11 - 13 cm**

(Tyrannus melancholicus)

Other names: Pepite. **Family:** Tyrannidae - Flycatchers. **Habitat:** Both humid and arid zones; open and semi open country with trees, river edges on forested zones, clearings, agricultural fields, gardens in towns and noisy cities. Avoid thickly forested areas. **Range:** From sw USA to all of South America except the w slope of the Andes in central Peru to the s. Up to 2700 m. **Similar species:** Myarchus tuberculifer.

Behavior: A bossy, bellicose bird with a stout bill. It guards quite ably its territory, chasing even hawks and other intruding big birds. Usually solitary, it perches in open treetops, snags or other exposed places, from where it sallies for insects at any height, including ground level or water. It pursues flying insects making spectacular sallies after them, in agile swooping flight. Usually returns to the same perch. Eats fruit too. Nest is a frail cup usually saddled on fork of a tree. Its song can be heard very early and it is very common. Seek for it around Puente Ruinas. **20 - 22 cm**

Big, Conspicuous Birds Inside the Forest

7

Andean Guan

(Penelope montagnii)

Other names: Pava andina, Pava de monte, Jachahuallpa.
Family: Cracidae - Guans. **Habitat:** Humid forests and borders with epyphytes; sometimes in isolated trees far from the woods. **Range:** Andes from nw Venezuela to nw Argentina. From 1800 to 3500 m.
Similar species: Chamaepetes goudotii.

Behavior: A large turkey-like bird with an erectile crest and strong feet and legs. Travels wary and quietly through the canopy or sub canopy of the woods forest, in groups of 3 to 7 members. Arboreal, it only comes down to ground level for fallen fruit or drinking. They are louder when breeding, and give a characteristic wing-whirring display at dawn. Nests are twigs and leaf platforms in a tree and the young can climb through foliage after a few days. Like most Cracidae members, the Andean Guam is considered a game bird. It can be found in forested areas throughout the MPHS. **60 cm**

(Piaya cayana)

Other names: Cuco ardilla, Arriero. **Family:** Cuculidae - Cuckoos, Anis.
Habitat: Dry to wet forests, forest borders, and semi open areas with trees.
Range: From w Mexico to n Argentina and Uruguay, including the entire Amazon basin. Up to 2700 m. **Similar species:** Coccyzus melacoryphus.

Behavior: Owes its name to its colour, its long tail and its moves upon the trees. Often unobtrusive, hops through thick vegetation and vine tangle in a series of leaping bounds that resemble a squirrel, then glides across a clearing. It occurs alone, in pairs or among mixed flock. Eats large insects, ants and caterpillars. Its nest is a frail platform in the forked branch of a bush or tree. It can be seen along the Urubamba River. **40 - 43 cm**

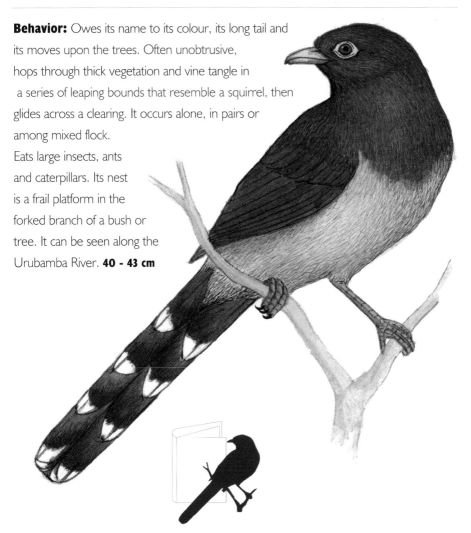

(Pharomachrus antisianus)

Other names: Quetzal. **Family:** Trogonidae - Trogons, Quetzals. **Habitat:** Humid forests and forest edges with abundant epiphytes and moss. **Range:** E slope of the Andes, from nw Venezuela to w Bolivia. From 1100 to 3000 m.

Behavior: Like all quetzals, it is notorious for its metallic colours and the elongated wings and tail. Generally solitary, it perches high up in dense foliage, upright and motionless for long periods, most often in fruiting trees. Their sallies are either hovering momentarily to pluck fruit, or swooping to catch insects on the wing. It nests in tree holes, woodpecker holes or old termite nests. Search for it around the Puente Ruinas bridge. **33 cm**

(Pharomachrus auriceps)

Other names: Quetzal. **Family:** Trogonidae - Trogons, Quetzals. **Habitat:** Same as the Crested Quetzal, but it covers a broader elevational range. **Range:** From Panama to w Bolivia. From 500 to 3100 m.

Behavior: In general terms, its behaviour is similar to the Crested quetzal, since both inhabit the same places. It can be seen along the Inca Trail. **34 cm**

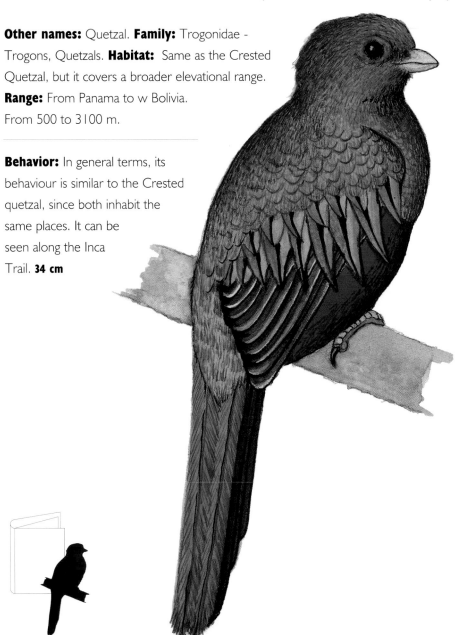

(Trogon personatus)

Other names: Canaura. **Family:** Trogonidae - Trogons, Quetzals.
Habitat: Humid forests and forest edges.
Range: From Venezuela and Guyana to w Bolivia. From 700 to 3600 m.

Behavior: Like the other species of Trogonidae, it is a highly colourful bird with a long tail. Often solitary, it can also be seen in pairs or family groups. It is a bit sluggish; it often perches quietly and upright for long periods in the

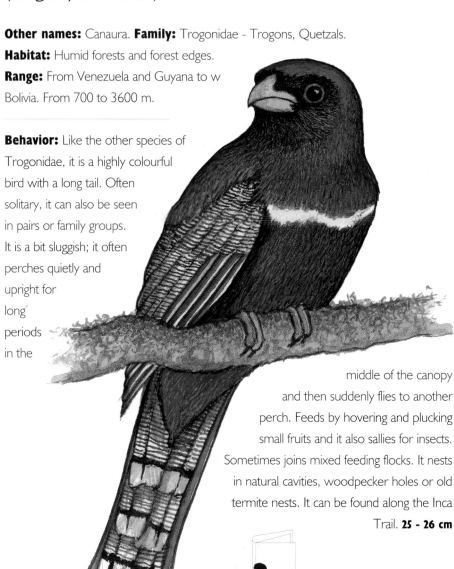

middle of the canopy and then suddenly flies to another perch. Feeds by hovering and plucking small fruits and it also sallies for insects. Sometimes joins mixed feeding flocks. It nests in natural cavities, woodpecker holes or old termite nests. It can be found along the Inca Trail. **25 - 26 cm**

(Momotus aequatorialis)

Other names: Relojero. **Family:** Momotidae - Motmots. **Habitat:** Humid forests, forest edges, glades, thickets, lighter woodland, gardens; never inside tall forests.
Range: Andes from Colombia to e Peru.
From 1500 to 2400 m.

Behavior: A very colourful, sluggish and inconspicuous bird. Perches alone or in pairs, often along streamside boulders, at mid level parts of the tree. Seats motionless, but every so often swings its tail from side to side like a clock, hence the Spanish name "Relojero" (clock maker). It sallies abruptly to foliage, branches or ground for prey. It is omnivorous: eats insects, small mammals, fruit, etc. It is more active at dawn or late afternoon and has an owl-like call. Their nests are burrows. It is common along the Urubamba River, near Aguas Calientes. **48 cm**

Golden-olive Woodpecker

(Piculus rubiginosus)

Other names: Carpintero **Family:** Picidae - Woodpeckers, Pájaros Carpinteros. **Habitat:** Humid forests and borders; heavy, tall forests; also in dry forests of Peruvian w slope of the Andes. **Range:** From Mexico to n Argentina. From 1000 to 3000 m. **Similar species:** P. rivolii.

Behavior: Usually a single bird, it moves slowly and quietly at mid level or in the forest's canopy. Like the rest of its family, it has a strong beak and a stretching tongue, specially fit for extracting bugs out of wood or the bark of trees. It forages by tapping and chiselling on limbs, branches and vines, or by probing into mossy limbs. Usually follows mixed flocks. They nest in holes excavated in trees. It can be found near the Puente Ruinas bridge.

23 cm

(Aulacorhynchus prasinus)

Other names: Tucaneta **Family:** Ramphastidae - Toucans. **Habitat:** Humid forests, forest edges, lighter woodland, man made clearings. **Range:** From s Mexico to w Venezuela and the Andes down to nw Bolivia. From 800 to 3700 m.
Similar species: A. coeruleicinctus, Andigena hypoglauca.

Behavior: Like all toucans, it has an enormous bill. It is rather active, elusive, noisy and sometimes inquisitive.

They happen in pairs or small groups at all levels of the forest. Often seen moving in a line, following the leader, at the higher levels of the foliage. It is omnivorous: eats fruit, insects, small invertebrates and other birds' eggs and nestlings. It nests in hollow trees. In the MPHS it can be seen in the lower Mandor Valley and the Aobamba Valley.

30 - 34 cm, including bill's length

Red-crested Cotinga

(Ampelion rubrocristatus)

Other names: Cotinga. **Family:** Cotingidae - Cotingas. **Habitat:** Humid forests; forest borders, clearing, hedgerows, agricultural areas with scattered trees, Polylepis forests. **Range:** The Andes from w Venezuela to nw Bolivia. From 2500 to 3700 m. **Similar species:** A. rufaxilla.

Behavior: A sluggish, arboreal bird. It occurs in pairs perching upright near or at the top of bushes and trees. More often than not, it allows people to get a close look. It can stay motionless for a long while, turning the head occasionally and looking around nervously. Eats fruits and insects that it catches making high, vertical sallies from the treetops. During displays and disputes, two birds will face one another with raised crest and fanned tail, flicking the wings and bobbing the head while calling. Their nest is a lichen cup in a small tree or shrub. It is monogamous and only the female incubates, but both parents feed the young. It is common along the Inca Trail. **21 - 23 cm**

(Pipreola intermedia)

Other names: Verdecito. **Family:** Cotingidae - Cotingas. **Habitat:** Humid forests, cloud forests, forest borders, occasionally outside the woods on a fruiting tree.
Range: E slope of the Peruvian Andes and w Bolivia. From 2000 to 3000 m.
Similar species: P. pulchra.

Behavior: A plump, notably lethargic arboreal bird. It happens alone or in pairs at the lower and middle levels in the thickest parts of the forest. Usually, they can be seen gathering at a fruiting tree. It can stay motionless for a long time. Like other Pipreola, eats mostly fruit and very seldom insects. It is monogamous and, same as other species of Cotingidae, only the female incubates, although both parents feed the young. **19 cm**

(Rupicola peruviana)

Other names: Gallito de las Rocas, Zunga. **Family:** Cotingidae - Cotingas. **Habitat:** Humid forested streams, wooded gorges, steep forested ravines and adjacent forest. **Range:** Andes from w Venezuela to nw Bolivia. From 500 to 2400 m.

Behavior: It is a wary and shy arboreal bird. Generally it stays within the forest at low or mid level, feeding on fruits, but it makes the occasional appearance in a clearing. In the breeding season, males perform noisy communal courtship displays, early in the morning and late in the afternoon. They face each other, bowing, jumping, bill snapping and flapping their wings on branches at middle vegetation. During the display, they extend the crest forward to cover the whole beak. Females watch the display and then chose a male. Females take care of all nesting duties. Nests are built with mud, stuck to the side of a dump rock face. It is the National Bird of Peru. It can be watched along railway tracks between the Puente Ruinas bridge and the Mandor Valley. **31 cm**

(Psarocolius atrovirens)

Other names: Coeche. **Family:** Icterinae - Orioles. **Habitat:** Borders of humid forests and adjacent clearings with scattered trees, and along rivers and streams.
Range: E slopes of the Andes from s Peru to nw Bolivia. Mostly from 800 to 2400 m.
Similar species: P. angustifrons.

Behaviour: It is a noisy bird, noted for the complexity of its calls. It has a pale and sharply pointed bill. They move in flocks through the forest canopy, foraging berries and fruits. They also breed and roost together, so they nest in small colonies. Their nests are pendulum-like, beautifully woven, and hang down from the tree tops. The display rituals are somehow elaborate. It should be easy to find along the Urubamba River, downstream from Aguas Calientes. **41 cm**

Hummingbirds

(Boissonneaua matthewsii)

Other names: Picaflor. **Family:** Trochilidae - Hummingbirds. **Habitat:** Canopy and interior of humid forests; also forest edges. **Range:** From Colombia to e Peru. From 1200 to 2700 m.

Behavior: It is a notably aggressive and territorial bird. Defends its patches of flowers from midlevel to canopy. Several individuals may congregate at flowering trees. It holds up wings in "V" when it clings to flowers for feeding, or momentarily when alighting. It sucks nectar from flowers and also hawks for insects. It can be seen on the slopes of the Machu Picchu ruins and around Aguas Calientes.

II cm + a bill of I.8 cm

Collared Inca

(Coeligena torquata)

Other names: Gould`s Inca, Colibrí. **Family:** Trochilidae - Hummingbirds.
Habitat: Humid forests and shrubby forest borders. **Range:** Venezuela and the Andes to n Bolivia. From 1500 to 3000 m.

Behavior: An active and silent bird with long, straight, needle like bill. Darts and flashes through dense vegetation at low to middle heights. Its beak is adapted to suck nectar by hovering below pendant flowers with long corollas. It also hawks for insects. It may join mixed flocks. It nests under ferns in rocky cliffs. Can be watched along the railway tracks between Aguas Calientes and the Mandor valley. **11 cm + a bill of 3.3 cm**

(Colibri coruscans)

Other names: Colibrí. azul, Quenchito. **Family:** Trochilidae - Hummingbirds. **Habitat:** Mostly not too humid habitats; forest borders, dry open places with scattered trees, pastures, parks and gardens; flowering pisonay trees (Erythrina sp); common at highlands. **Range:** Mountains of Venezuela and the Andes down to nw Argentina. Mainly from 2000 to 3000 m, and up to 4500 in breeding season. **Similar species:** C. thalassinus.

Behavior: This active bird protects fiercely its territory and flowers, chasing away competitors with a fast buzzing attack. It is very dominant among hummingbirds. Feeds at all levels of the vegetation, sucking nectar from the upright as much as from the horizontal flowers. Sings from exposed bare twigs in the treetops. Their display flight is a steep few metres climb and a swoop back to the perch. It nests in trees. Very common throughout Peruvian Andes. To be watched along the Inca Trail and in most gardens in Cusco City. **13 cm + a bill of 2.5 cm**

(Lesbia nuna)

Other names: Picaflor.
Family: Trochilidae -
Hummingbirds. **Habitat:**
Shrubby forest borders, semi
humid scrub, bushy slopes and
ravines,
open areas with
scattered hedges,
parks and gardens. **Range:**
Andes from w Venezuela to w
Bolivia. From 1700 to 3800 m.
Similar species: L. victoriae.

Behavior: An active and aggressive bird of
short beak and long tail. Hovers for nectar at a
variety of flowers, from the lower level of the forest to
the highest in the canopy. It also catches insects. Their
flight is weaving and bee like, same as other small
hummingbirds. During display flight, male flies in a zigzag
pattern in front of his perched partner. It could be found
anywhere along the Inca Trail.

16 cm + a bill of 1 cm

(Leucippus viridicauda)

Other names: Picaflor. **Family:** Trochilidae - Hummingbirds. **Habitat:** Humid forests, forest edges, clearings, overgrown landslides, scrubs, fields, gardens; flowering Inga trees. **Range:** E slopes of the Peruvian central Andes. From 900 to 2800 m.
Similar species: L. chionogaster.

Behavior: It is a Peruvian endemic bird, and it has not been studied much. Feeds on the nectar of many flower species. Catches insects too. It sings from an exposed perch. It is common along the Urubamba River and around the town of Aguas Calientes. All the Hummingbirds beat their wings fast, which allows them to keep stationary in the air. They can also fly backwards. **8.5 cm + a bill of 2.5 cm**

Booted Racket-tail

(Ocreatus underwoodii)

Other names: Colibrí cola de hoja. **Family:** Trochilidae - Hummingbirds. **Habitat:** Humid forests, forest borders, glades, damp shady ravines; flowering Inga trees.
Range: Andes from Venezuela to s Bolivia. From 850 to 3100 m.

Behavior: A very small bird; the male has a long tail. It can be seen weaving in and out of the foliage, with a fast, beelike flight. Occurs alone at lower levels, but it usually gathers with other hummingbirds at the canopy of a wide variety of flowering trees. Hovers or clings to blossoms to suck nectar, uttering a soft, twittering call. Holds wings outstretched for a few seconds after alighting. Keeps feeding territories. Its nest is a downy cup atop twig. It can be seen at the Mandor Valley.

12 cm + a bill of 1.3 cm

(Patagona gigas)

Other names: Colibrí gigante, Quencho. **Family:** Trochilidae - Hummingbirds.

Habitat: Open arid areas of high Andes; dry tableland and canyons with shrubs, Agave and cactuses; agricultural fields, hedgerows, gardens. Avoids humid forests.

Range: Andes from Ecuador to s Chile. From 1000 to 4500 m.

Similar species: Ptereophanes cyanopterus.

Behavior: It is the world's largest hummingbird. When it is flying resembles a "swift" with a long bill or a "swallow". Flies and hovers with slow, bat like wing beats, slower than those of other hummingbirds. It is territorial and aggressive, chasing other species away from its feeding site. Hovers or perches to feed on nectar. It also hawks for insects. Builds a tiny nest, too small for its own size, on a branch, cactus stem or a cliff face. Look out for it along the Inca Trail. **19 cm + a bill of 4 cm**

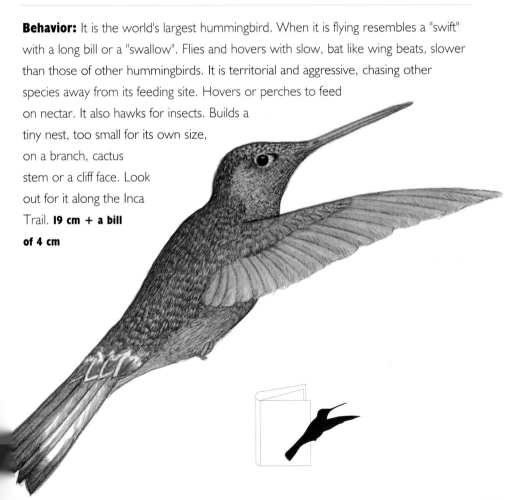

Small, Colored Birds Moving Active Through Foliage in the Forest

9

(Eubucco versicolor)

Other names: Eubuco. **Family:** Capitonidae - Barbets. **Habitat:** Humid forests and forest edges. **Range**: Andes of e Peru and w Bolivia. From 750 to 2500 m.

Behavior: A stocky bird with short neck and legs and a pale, conical heavy bill. It occurs alone or in pairs at mid levels of the forest, sometimes among mixed feeding flocks. Eats buds, blossoms, fruits and insects. It is very active when it forages, but it perches quietly. It nests in tree cavities.

16 cm

Ocellated Piculet

(Picumnus dorbygnianus)

Other names: Carpinterito **Family:** Picidae - Woodpeckers.
Habitat: Humid forests, tangles, forest with lots of epiphytes. **Range:** Andes of
e Peru, Bolivia and nw Argentina. From 1100 to 2500 m.

Behavior: It is a small woodpecker.
Appears singly or in pairs, often
accompanying mixed species flocks. Like all
members of its family, it has a strong bill and a
long barbed tongue, ideal for extracting insects
out of wood or the bark of trees. The beak is
also used for tapping "telegraph messages" and
communicate with other individuals. This bird is
fairly common along the road between
Aguas Calientes and the Mandor
Valley. **9 - 10 cm**

(Xenops rutilans)

Other names: Trepadorcito. **Family:** Furnariidae - Ovenbirds. **Habitat:** Humid forests, forest edges and lighter woodland. **Range:** From Costa Rica to Venezuela and the Andes to n Argentina, and s Brazil. Up to 2500 m. **Similar species:** Premnoplex brunnescens, Margarornis squamiger.

Behavior: Small, acrobatic, arboreal birds. It often hangs upside down. They move closely together in pairs or groups of three, at middle and canopy levels, as they follow a mixed flock. It forages for insects at lower levels by working along or beneath slender branches, swiveling from side to side and pecking and scraping dead wood and bark. They nest in natural or excavated cavities in trees. They are monogamous and both parents take care of the fledglings. You can find it along the railway tracks near Puente Ruinas.

II - I2 cm

(Pachyramphus versicolor)

Other names: Cabezón. **Family:** Tyrannidae - Tyrant Flycatchers. **Habitat:** Canopy and borders of humid forests, cloud forests and lighter woodland. **Range:** From Costa Rica to w Venezuela and the Andes to n Bolivia. Mostly from 1600 to 2600 m; occasionally to 3500 m.

Behavior: A common, chunky bird at Machu Picchu. It is fairly active. Frequently raises its crown feathers. Forages busily for insects at all levels of the vegetation, singly or in pairs, and sometimes in mixed species flocks. Hovers and flits at foliage or hops along branches. It also eats fruit. The nests are rounded woven structures in trees. Common in the humid forest areas of the MPHS. **13 cm**

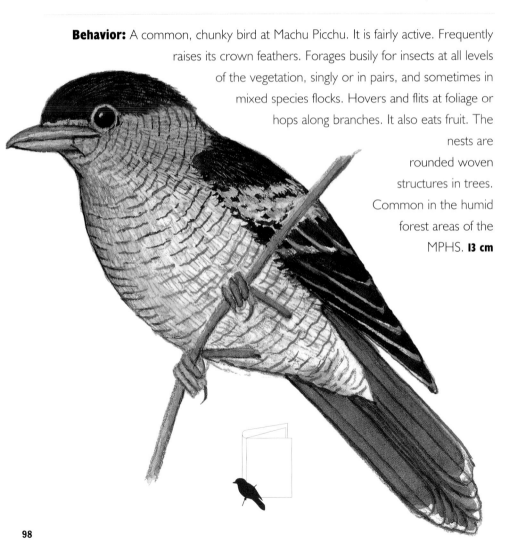

(Todirostrum cinereum)

Other names: Espatulilla. **Family:** Tyrannidae - Tyrant Flycatchers. **Habitat:** Shrubby clearings, forest borders, lighter woodland, thickets, hedgerows and gardens. Avoids dense forests and arid regions. **Range:** From s Mexico to Venezuela and Guyana; e slopes of the Andes down to Bolivia; all over Brazil except at the core of Amazonia. Up to 2000 m.

Behavior: A bold and active bird with long, flattened, spatula-like bill. Usually found in pairs, they move through thick foliage fluttering and hopping about, with the tail perpetually cocked over back. In a common display it hitches along a branch. It also sallies for flying prey. It is permanently in motion and often looks almost comical. It builds a pendant, globular nest on trees. You can watch it between Aguas Calientes and Puente Ruinas. **9.5 cm**

(Thryothorus eisenmanni)

Other names: Cucarachero. **Family:** Troglodytidae - Wrens. **Habitat**: Borders of humid forests, specially where bamboo stems are abundant. **Range:** A bird endemic to Peru, it only exists in the area of Machu Picchu and its surroundings. From 1800 to 3400 m. **Similar species:** Henicorhina leucophrys.

Behavior: This endemic bird from Cusco was described to scientists as recently as 1974. It is a handsome, active bird that happens in pairs or family groups, never joining mixed flocks. Forages for insects probing at scrubs and bamboo stem clusters. It builds dome shaped nests. It can be seen wherever there are stands of bamboo in the ruins grounds, and its song is a characteristic sound of Machu Picchu. **15 - 16 cm**

(Basileuterus coronatus)

Other names: Reinita. **Family:** Parulinae - Wood Warblers. **Habitat:** Lower growth of humid forests, cloud forests and forest borders. **Range:** nw Venezuela and the Andes to w Peru and nw Bolivia. From 1400 to 2800 m. **Similar species:** B. fulvicauda.

Behavior: Forages actively near the ground, in pairs or in family groups, hopping in foliage and gleaning from tree trunks and branches. It also joins mixed flocks. Its charming song, sung by the male, can be frequently heard. The female builds the nest and incubates, but both parents feed the young. It nests in banks. It can be seen along the Urubamba River between Aguas Calientes and the Aobamba Valley. **14 - 15 cm**

(*Myioborus miniatus*)

Other names: Candelita. **Family:** Parulinae - Wood Warblers. **Habitat:** Humid forests, cloud forests, borders and lighter woodland; tolerates well some perturbed habitats. **Range:** From Mexico to Venezuela and Guyana; the Andes from Colombia to s Bolivia. Mostly from 700 to 2500 m. **Similar species:** M. melanocephalus.

Behavior: It is a very common, conspicuous and extremely active bird. Feeds on insects, mostly at mid to high levels. Occurs in pairs, in family groups or with mixed flocks. Sallies short distances acrobatically, hops along high or low branches or clings to vines or trunks. Often postures with its wings drooped and its tail spread like a fan, and wags its body from side to side. Its song is often heard. The female builds the nest and incubates, but both parents feed the young. It nests in banks. It is common in Machu Picchu and can be seen along the railway tracks between Aguas Calientes and the Mandor Valley. **13 cm**

(Thraupis bonariensis)

Other names: Pichaco, Naranjero. **Family:** Thraupinae - Tanagers.

Habitat: Prefers semiarid areas; lighter woodland and scrubby hillsides with cactuses; agricultural areas and gardens with trees and shrubs. **Range:** Andes of Ecuador to w Bolivia, Paraguay, Uruguay and ne Argentina. Up to 3600 m.

Behavior: Active, conspicuous and noisy like all Thraupis tanagers. Aggressive too. It occurs alone, in pairs or family groups. When not disturbed, is a tame bird and it allows a very close look while foraging from low levels to tree tops. Flies in swift undulating flight. It feeds on fruits and leaves. Often seen at cactus fruits. It could cause great damages to cultivated fruit trees. It nests high in trees or cactuses. It can be found along the Inca Trail.

17 - 18 cm

(Thraupis cyanocephala)

Other names: Azulejo. **Family:** Thraupinae - Tanagers. **Habitat:** Humid forests, shrubby forest borders and openings, overgrown pastures, regenerating areas, hedges; areas with alder trees (Alnus sp); rarely inside continuous forest. **Range:** Mountains of Venezuela and in the Andes down to Bolivia. Mostly from 1400 to 3000 m

Behavior: Active, conspicuous and noisy bird, like all Thraupis tanagers, but it can sit motionless for a while. It happens in pairs or small groups, sometimes with mixed flocks, foraging for fruit at all levels and sometimes fly catching upwards. Perches in the open on tops of shrubs or trees. The nest is an open cup on trees. It is common along the road between the Machu Picchu ruins and the Puente Ruinas bridge. **16 - 18 cm**

(Thraupis episcopus)

Other names: Violinista, Luisa. **Family:** Thraupinae - Tanagers. **Habitat:** All kinds of non-forested, dry and humid habitats; forest and river edges, settled and deforested areas, plantations, fields, parks, gardens, trees and shrubbery in agricultural areas.
Range: From Mexico to n Bolivia and n Amazonian Brazil. Up to 2600 m.
Similar species: T. palmarum.

Behavior: A noisy, energetic, bold bird, very tolerant of human habitats. It is sociable and occurs in pairs or small groups. Basically arboreal, it may forage anywhere. Feeds at all levels, on a wide variety of fruits, including those of cultivated plants; it is quite versatile when it forages, as it peers head down along branches and gleans foliage. It also catches insects in flight. It builds a thick, deep cup nest at trees. Its range is expanding due to deforestation and agricultural settlement. It is more common in the lowlands but it can be easily found around Aguas Calientes. **16 cm**

Beryl-spangled Tanager

(Tangara nigroviridis)

Other names: Tangara mariposa. **Family:** Thraupinae - Tanagers. **Habitat:** Humid forests, specially forest borders, clearings with scattered tall trees. **Range:** Mountains of Venezuela and the Andes to n Bolivia. Mostly from 1500 to 2500 m.

Behavior: It forages at mid to high levels and sometimes near the ground. Notably frugivorous, it moves fast picking berries or insects from leaves, and gleans and peers at bare twigs. Occurs in pairs or groups which frequently associate with mixed species flocks. Nests are open cups placed on trees. You can watch this bird along the Urubamba River between Aguas Calientes and the Mandor Valley.

13 cm

(Tangara ruficervix)

Other names: Tangara dorada. **Family:** Thraupinae - Tanagers. **Habitat:** Inside tall humid forests, forest borders, shrubby regenerating clearings, isolated tall trees. **Range:** The Andes from Colombia to nw Bolivia. Mostly from 1500 to 2400 m. **Similar species:** T. vassorii.

Behavior: Eats a lot of fruit and it forages for insects at mid to upper levels, searching limbs and clusters, gleaning on foliage and among twigs. Frequently peers under branches. Likes Cecropia tree catkins. It moves fast. Occurs in pairs, small groups or accompanying mixed flocks of other tanagers. Often perches fairly high. Nests are open cups placed on trees. It can be watched around the Puente Ruinas bridge. **13 cm**

(Tangara viridicollis)

Other names: Silvery Tanager, Tangara plateada.
Family: Thraupinae - Tanagers.
Habitat: Humid forests; cloud forests and forest borders, shrubby regenerating clearings, wooded ravines and gardens. **Range:** Andes from s Ecuador to e Peru. From 500 to 2700 m.

Behavior: An active, flocking bird , brightly colored like all tanagers. Eats fruits and searches for insects from the top of small trees to low bushes, and in the scrub on hillsides. They occur in pairs or small groups, or with mixed feeding flocks. Nests are open cups placed on trees. Very common along the Urubamba River around Puente Ruinas. **13 cm**

(Tangara xanthocephala)

Other names: Tangara cola amarilla.**Family:** Thraupinae
- Tanagers. **Habitat:** Humid forests and borders,
clearings with scattered large trees.
Range: Andes from Venezuela to nw Bolivia.
From 1300 to 2600 m.
Similar species: T. parzudakii.

Behavior: One of the most
frugivorous tanager, it forages in
the semi open, on twigs,
smaller branches and limbs,
often hanging and peering
under branches, at middle
to upper level. Eats
insects too. It occurs in
pairs or groups and
often in mixed flocks of
other tanagers.
Generally, it avoids
getting inside the woods.
Nests are open cups
placed on trees. It is a
familiar tanager at Machu
Picchu. **13 cm**

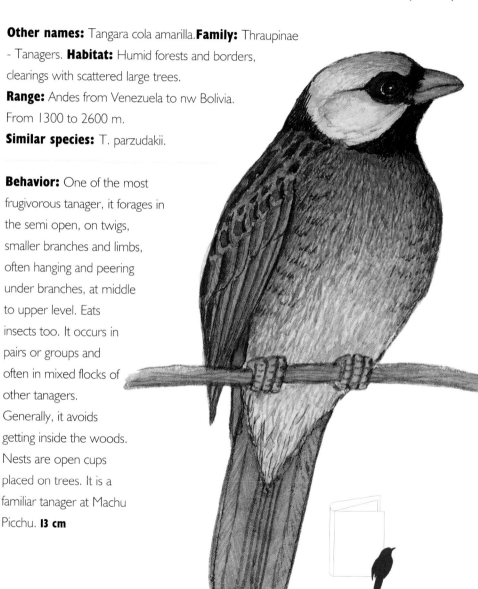

Glossary

Aguas Calientes: (literally, Hot Waters) Name given to the village of "Machu Picchu", to avoid confusing it with the ancient citadel's ruins.

Agave: Genus of a succulent plant called Maguey, which grows in the dry mountainsides. Its flowering stem reaches the 6 m height.

Alder (Alnus sp): Aliso. A tree that grows in creeks, near the streams.

Aobamba Valley: The Aobamba River flows onto the Urubamba River precisely where the latter exits the MPHS boundaries. This is also the least elevated spot in the Sanctuary (1725 m above sea level).

Canopy: The upper part of the treetops or forest.

Capuli (Prunus sp): A tree cultivated in the valleys. Its fruit is a berry, edible for birds as well as for man.

Cecropia: Genus of a tree commonly called Cetico, notable for having great hand shaped leaves. It grows in humid forests.

Display: Set movements or "dances" that birds perform in breeding season aimed at impressing and attracting the females. There are some aggression displays too, against a rival or competitor.

Epiphytes: Plants that grow on trunks, tree branches or other plants.

Eucalyptus: Exotic tree, introduced in Peru in the nineteenth century. It is very common in the Andes.

Glean: To garner, to pick and choose, to collect. It refers to the action of moving through the foliage searching and selecting prey; perch-gleaning is when it picks and chooses insects without moving from its perch; sally-gleaning or hover-gleaning is when it catches insects in flight.

Inca Trail: Ancient Inca Pathway that leads to the citadel of Machu Picchu, used today by hikers from all over the world. It is a 4 days walk.

Inga: Genus of a great number of species of trees, commonly called Pacae.

Llactapata ruins: One of the many Inca

ruins found along the Inca Trail (approximate elevation is 2600 m).

Mandor valley: The Mandor River joins the Urubamba River downstream from the town of Aguas Calientes.

Molle (Schinus sp): A common tree in the Andean valleys and in semi arid slopes.

MPHS: Machu Picchu Historical Sanctuary.

N, s, e, w: north, south, east, west.

Pisonay (Erythrina sp): Tree that grows in mountainous tropical forest; very nice looking, thanks to its bright red flowers.

Polylepis: Genus of the tree locally known as Queñua. Very resistant to cold temperatures, it is common in the Andes highlands.

Puente Ruinas: (Ruins Bridge) Bridge over the Urubamba River, downstream from the village of Aguas Calientes, leading to the Machu Picchu ruins.

Puna: Name given to the highlands region of the Andes, above the 4000 m elevation, covered by coarse grasses known as "ichu" and nearly bare of bushes.

Sally, sallies: Outings, to go out; it refers to short flights made by birds to catch some prey, turning back quickly to a safe perch.

Stoop: The particular way in which falcons dive over their prey.

Tierra del Fuego: (literally, Land of Fire) Archipelago in the southernmost point of the South American Continent.

Urubamba River: A river of the Amazon basin. Important because it flows all along the Sacred Valley of the Incas, where there is plenty of remaining Inca structures.

Wallabamba: Ancient Villa in the Inca Trail (approximate elevation 2900 m).

Willows (Salix sp): Sauce. A common tree in the Andean valleys. It usually grows in riverbanks or streamsides.

Index

Bibliography

CANADAY, Chris; JOST, Lou. (1997). *Common Birds of Amazonian Ecuador: a guide for the wide-eyed ecotourist.* Ediciones Libri Mundi. Quito.

CLEMENTS, James F.; SHANY, Noam. (2001). *A Field Guide to the Birds of Peru.* Ibis Publishing Company. Temecula, California.

FJELDSA, Jon; KRABBE, Niels. (1990). *Birds of the High Andes.* Zoological Museum, University of Copenhagen.

FROST, Peter; BARTLE, Jim. (1995). *Santuario Histórico Machu Picchu.* Editorial Nuevas Imágenes. Lima.

GALIANO SÁNCHEZ, Washington. (2000). *Situación Ecológico-Ambiental del Santuario Histórico de Machu Picchu: Una Aproximación.* PROFONAMPE-Programa Machu Picchu. Cusco.

GONZALES, Oscar; PAUTRAT, Lucila; GONZALES, José. (1998). *Las Aves mas Comunes de Lima y sus Alrededores.* Grupo de Aves del Perú. Editorial Santillana. Lima.

HARRISON, Colin; GREENSMITH, Alan. (1993). *Birds of the World.* D. K. Publishing Inc. New York.

HILTY, Steven L.; BROWN, William L. (1986). *Birds of Colombia.* Princeton University Press. Princeton, New Jersey.

KOEPCKE, María. (1964). *Las Aves del Departamento de Lima.* Lima.

KOEPCKE, Hans; KOEPCKE, María. (1963). *Las Aves Silvestres de Importancia Económica del Perú.* Ministerio de Agricultura, Lima.

NATIONAL GEOGRAPHIC SOCIETY. (2002). *Birds of North America.* National Geographic Society. Washington D.C.

PULIDO CAPURRO, Victor. (1998). *Vocabulario de los Nombres Comunes de la Fauna Silvestre del Perú.* Lima.

RIDGELY, Robert S; TUDOR Guy. (2001). *The Birds of South America.* World Wildlife Fund; William L. Brown; University of Texas Press. Austin.

STOTZ F. Douglas; et al. (1996). *Neotropical Birds: Ecology and Conservation.* Conservation International and The Field Museum of Natural History; University of Chicago Press. Chicago and London.

WALKER, Barry; FJELDSA, Jon. (2001). *Field Guide to the Birds of Machu Picchu.* Profonanpe-Programa Machu Picchu. Cusco.

GINO CASSINELLI was born in Lima. He is a forestry engineer from the Universidad Nacional Agraria de La Molina (National Agrarian University at La Molina, Lima) and has pursued studies in Mining and Environment in the Universidad Nacional de Ingeniería (National Engineering University) in Lima. In 1996 he started taking photographs of the vegetation in the Cusco area, aiming to elaborate tourist field guides about Nature. Before this book, he has published "Trees and Bushes from the Sacred Valley of the Incas", currently available in its second edition.

DANIEL HUAMAN is a Biologist graduated in the Universidad Nacional Agraria La Molina (National Agrarian University at La Molina, Lima).

This work has been revised by Alfredo Begazo and Thomas Valqui Haase; both recognized Peruvian Ornithologists, with extensive knowledge of the Country's territory.